Shadows from Behind
A Memoir

Imani Aester

Shadows from Behind
ISBN: 978-1-7367455-7-1
Copyright ©2021 by Imani Aestar
All rights reserved. No part of this book may be reproduced in any form whatsoever, including information storage and retrieval systems, without permission in writing from the author—exceptions by reviewers, who may quote brief passages in a book review.

Edited by Shawn Jackson
Illustration by Yuly Raquel
Cover by Design Place LLC
Published by One2Mpower Publishing LLC

Introduction

This book started out as a way of therapy for me. Jotting my thoughts down in a Composition notebook, writing out my fears, struggles, disappointments in life, as well as accomplishments. But as I was writing, I saw something much more. A message could come out of my story. For you who are reading this book, come into my world and get a glimpse of my life, letting you know that you are not alone.

SHADOWS FROM BEHIND

Chapter 1
Earliest Memories

I just received a text from my sixteen-year-old daughter *Baby Girl*, saying she missed me, and I can tell through the multiple texts she was sending she is tired of running but scared of the consequences she will face **because of the choices she made growing up too fast to soon, running away because she doesn't want to follow the rules.** I often think of where I went wrong since I came from a dysfunctional background. But at the end of the day, we all have our own path to take. I struggled through some things like Jesus, Trinity, Allah, Muhammad, etc. Sometimes, I believe in Jesus. Sometimes, Islam. Lord, help my struggles. I'm weak. My spirit is weak again! I don't know how to deal with it. Here we go again. I missed Baby Girl all the time. My husband, Darrell, is trying to hold us all together, but he is suffering too because he does not have anyone to talk to about his issues. I don't know what to do. We practice what we preach...okay...we practice what we preach! Then I think, *it's all good,* over and over again, trying to make myself feel good. But I'm fooling myself. Who knows that we don't practice what we preach, and everything is not *all good.* Sitting here, saying, *help us, Lord. Help us, Lord.* Sitting here worrying about my children.

Wow, as I lay here on the bed wondering what happened, I took a moment as my mind drifted back to my earliest memories of my childhood. I was four years old; I remember my mother had me by my hand as my aunt on my father's side was crying as she and my mother were going back and forth arguing. I remember looking back as my mother walked me away. The farther we walked, the more distance came between my auntie and me, my favorite auntie. I didn't see her or my father's side of the family for some time. I remember not understanding until later in life. At times, I looked at my mother and saw sadness in her eyes. I remember when there were times when we stayed at rooming houses. The fire, the smoke, my mother's voice. God had his hands on us. We made it. Alhamdulillah. Going back and forth to visit my stepfather in prison. Remembering getting up early in the morning riding the subway, laying on my mother's lap as I fell asleep. The coldness of winter in New Jersey but loving the warmth of a mother's touch.

    I remember having my veil (hijab) on, also Mother, as she was practicing Islam and raised my siblings and me in Islam too. Mother let me start going over to visit my biological father and his family around the age of six years old. At this time, she was married to my stepdad, Wali. Guardian and my other siblings, all his biological children, came into the picture. I used to love seeing my dad, Big Daddy, Big Mama, Auntie, and my uncles. Remembering the hugs and kisses, the combing of my hair. "Ouch!" I used to say to Auntie. Remembering when my dad used to pick me up, or my mother used to drop me off. Enjoying and feeling loved until the incident that changed everything.

    My father and his girlfriend were going to visit my uncle, my daddy's brother. It was the weekend I came over. My dad kept on telling me to lie down on the seat as we were riding. Me being young, I wanted to see what they were doing in the front seat, and by the way, something was stinking. My stomach was aching. I felted like I had to throw up. Well, as I looked over the seat, I saw my dad putting something green, looked like grass, into pink balloons and tying them up as they went. I didn't know then what I know now what they were doing—smuggling weed into the prison. I told Mother, and that was the last time I saw my dad until later in my life. I remember feeling lost, like it was my fault I told on my dad, and now I can't see my dad or Big Daddy, Big Mama, or my favorite aunt. That's when my life started to change.

    I can remember my father knocking at my mother's door and she telling me to go upstairs and don't make a sound as she and my father went back and forth about him seeing me. At that age, I wanted to run downstairs and say, "Daddy, I'm here," but I was scared I was going to get in trouble.

Remembering when my father brought me a bike and Mother didn't want me to have it. In fact, she gave it away.

I didn't have a typical childhood. There were good times as well as bad times. I can remember my mother and my siblings, at this time, I was the oldest of six siblings, going to the mosque. Remembering Eid Mubarak, the Muslim celebration twice yearly.

Remembering my mother sewing clothes and cutting out patterns because she didn't want us to wear of the world clothing. The smell of mac and cheese from scratch and oxtails, but I can't help but not to remember my mind going back to the words, "I wish you were never born" or "I should have aborted you. You will never amount to shit!" As a grown woman, those words are still in the back of my head. As I look back on my life, I often said to myself, "Little Muff, we are going to be okay."

Mother took me out of school when I was in the fifth grade. I remember her saying she would home school me, which never happened. At this time, my stepfather was over in the Middle East on a student visa. We went to join him as a family. I can remember I was around ten- or eleven-years old boarding Saudi Airlines. Boy, it was a long trip dressed in all black getting off the plane. Living in the Middle East wasn't bad at all. Besides, in the 1980's we lived in a little apartment. I remember cockroaches, lizards, goats, chickens, and rats. I used to go to the Holy Mosque Al-Haram. We frequently drunk Zamzam water; it tasted different.

There were good and bad times overseas. Ultimately, Mother and the family moved back to the USA. Wow! A year went past. Let me stop. This is when life just got real—no good memories. But I'm strong. I can do this! I can tell my story. I must press forward to help others.

Chapter 2
Remembering

It was 1986 back in New Jersey, Camden, to be exact, living in Pollock Town on Thurman Ave. I remember it was a Polish woman, an elderly lady, that stayed next door to us. Mother going through it with my stepdad, now on her seventh child, doing what she had to do to hold it down. I was twelve years old, still not in school, basically helping Mother with my siblings in between still playing with dolls and pre-teenage, saying to myself, *what about me?* I felt lost. Have Mother tell it, I was a terrible child, on the phone talking about me to her friends. It always felt like my mother's friends' kids she praised but always put me down. It got to a point in my young life, well in Islam, when a girl comes on her period (menstruation), they are considered a woman. Mother was talking about marriage. Marrying me off ASAP! Can you imagine me hearing this from my mother? I knew she didn't like me. Well, that's what I felt. First, taking me from my father, my other part of my identity, now she wanted to take me away from her and my siblings? I didn't have any friends. I remember Mother told me if I ran away, she would beat me, and DFACS would take me away; so, I was totally helpless.

Mother had some Muslim men that she introduced me to, all much older than me, one in particular she knew. I remember her saying to him, "She looks like me, but she does not have hair like my other girls." Funny, I had a hair complex about my hair texture being of African American descent from my father's side. My mother's mother, my grandmother, is from Turkey. I didn't get that texture.

Mother used to cut all my hair off when I was younger up until eleven years old. She said she didn't know what to with my hair. I always felt like I was punished for something I couldn't control. Well, he used to come over to talk to me, and Mother used to leave him alone with me. One night, I remember being downstairs, and we were lying down, and he started touching me down below. I remember feeling scared, ashamed, all alone. I guess he felt some kind of way, so he stopped. Well, I never told Mother. I wanted to protect her, and that didn't go anywhere because he was already married.

Through the verbal, emotional, and physical abuse and not going to school, I had enough! I finally had the courage to run away from home. I often thought about my father and grandparents, wondering if they knew where I was. One day, my mother left home. She told me to watch my siblings while she went to handle some business. When she left, I was so scared to leave, I didn't want to leave my siblings by themselves, but twelve years old, I had to make a move. So, I wrote Mother a letter letting her know that I left.

I remember leaving the house running, trying to get to the bus stop to get to my Big Mama and Big Daddy's home. I got on the bus scared, trying to picture the street and house. I saw that street and got off the bus and walked up and down the block asking people where the Maddox's stay? Finally, someone answered my cries and pointed me in the right direction. I walked up on the porch happy and nervous at the same time, knocked on the door, and I heard a women's voice ask, "Who is it?" I said, "Muffin," and the door opened. It was my Big Mama. She started crying, and I did too. My Big Daddy came to the door also. They took me into the house and asked me many questions. "Where have you been? Where is your mother? and Why am I here?" I told them Mother was trying to marry me off, and they lost it! They were trying to get back in contact with my father, but about the time my dad came, Mother showed up. See, when I wrote the letter telling her I was running away, I also said, "Don't worry about me, I'm going to my grandparents' house." Thinking about it now, Boy, did I mess up, but I know now God is in control of situations, and things happen for a reason.

    Well, Mother showed up and said

what she said. Remembering my grandparents crying as my mother took me away. I was so scared she was going to kill me, but she took me home. She said she was not going to touch me, but "If I ran away again, she was going to give me to DFACS." Well, I had so much fear in me I never ran again. That's when she really started looking for a husband for me.

SHADOWS FROM BEHIND

Chapter 3
The Hunt for a Husband

As time passed, Mother had an Islamic Horizon magazine. I remember Mother telling me I found a man from Somalia, and she talked to him on the phone. All I knew, she sent a picture of me to him, and he sent a picture of him to her. I talked to him twice, and the next thing I knew Mother, my stepfather, and I were flying to California. In Islam, it's a dowry, a gift from the groom to the bride. Well, I never saw this gift. I was thirteen years old going to another state to a man older than I that I don't know to get married. I didn't know how to think at this point in my life. I knew I was alone. It was about survival.

Arriving in California, all I remember is meeting with my soon-to-be husband, having the wedding, the women in one room and the men in the other. The person who married us asking, "Do I consent to this marriage," and my mother looking at me, giving me a look of *I wish the fuck you would go against me.* So, I said, "Yes." After that was over, my mother took me to the home where he stayed, a small studio in San Luis Obispo. I can remember being scared, nervous, feeling like I wanted to throw up. Mother was getting me ready for him, my wedding night.

Mother put me on a black lingerie lace top. I remember feeling awkward because it was see-through. I didn't want him to see my naked breast and red lipstick. Mother told me I'm going to be okay and kissed me on the forehead, and said, "Call me in the morning and tell me how it went." I heard a knock on the bedroom door. It was Husband. By me being a virgin, I was very nervous. In my mind, I just wanted my mother.

I remember laying down on the bed, and my body tensed up, hoping he didn't touch me. Well, he did. I began to cry while he was preparing my vagina with KY Jelly. I guess he saw how much pain I was in, so he stopped. I tried to fight him off for as long as I could. About a month into marriage, I gave in. Mother and Stepfather stayed in

California for about a week in order for me to be legally married. Because I was a minor, Mother had to sign her parental rights over to my husband. We talked on the phone, and I just wanted to go home, back to New Jersey. My innocence was taken. I was a wife at the age of thirteen.

    I didn't love this man, how I can love someone, get to know someone. I was thirteen years old, still watching videos, drawing, dancing, things that normal teenage girls do, although Mother raised me on the domestic side. I remember thinking, "How can my mother be so cruel." My mother, the woman that gave birth to me. I was devastated.

    Well, I was a wife, so I had to put my big panties on and move on. I had two children out of that marriage, a daughter and a son. My daughter I had when I was fifteen, and my son when I was seventeen years of age. I was married from the age thirteen to eighteen years of age from 1987 to 1993. I saw Mother. Well, in between the years, I visited my family in New Jersey.

After I had my first child, my husband sent me back home for the summer to visit. I stayed the summer with my mother and siblings. It felt good to be home. Mother acted like everything was good. I had so much hurt inside, my other siblings living normal lives, while my life was gone at that point.

Mother on her ninth child, my daughter was the same age as my youngest brother. Mother and Stepfather were on the verge of divorce at that time. I remember Mother crying, sitting on the floor while nursing my baby brother. She looked so sad, I didn't know what was wrong, but I just wanted her to smile. Well, in between the visit, I was out with Mother. She went to the store to get some groceries. While I was standing outside waiting on her, guess who I ran into? My biological father, who I hadn't seen since I was seven or eight years old. I couldn't believe it! Father called me by my nickname, Muffin, and said, "Is it you?" I replied,

"Yes."

I began to walk toward him slowly. He said, "It's okay, Muff." So, I ran to him so happy. Father asked me where had I been? He heard my mother took me overseas, came back, and then sold me to an Arab man. At that time, Father took me around the corner. As I was walking, Mother came out of the store and called my father by his name and asked, "What are you doing?" Well, they exchanged words, and he continued to talk to me. I had my baby girl with me. He told me he was so sorry when I ran away. Father further explained Big Mama called him, telling him I was there, but by the time he arrived, Mother had already taken me home. Father asked why I didn't run away again. At that time, Mother told me to come on. That was the last time I saw my father.

Well, I went back to California, continued my life as best as I knew how. Husband enrolled me in a community college there. I felt a little independent at this point. I had my second child, my son. I wanted desperately to get out of the marriage. I had no one to talk to. Mother had gone back to Saudi Arabia with my siblings. It was me against the world, so one day, I got up enough courage to tell my husband I didn't want to be married anymore. At this point in our marriage, Husband had sent for the rest of his family from Somalia.

    I moved into an apartment I shared with a roommate. Husband brought me my babies to visit, and I went over to his home to visit our kids, but one day, Husband took me to an African lawyer and had me sign papers. Not knowing I had signed all my parental rights over, giving him total custody of my kids. That was the turning point. No kids, no mother, I didn't know how to get in contact with her. My ex-husband moved, I dropped out of school. Homeless. That's when I turned away from Islam. I hated being Muslim. I felt why would Allah do this to me. If only I knew what I know now. So, I mixed up with the "C" life, gang life, and then I met this guy. I didn't know he was a pimp.

Chapter 4
Then Came A Pimp

After leaving the gang life and being raped by an OG set-up, I was still homeless, jumping from house to house. Friends that were not my friends, sneaking me in and out of their homes while their parents were at work or sleep. Friends saying, "They got my back." But we know what's that about, a favor for a favor.

A guy friend I was dealing with hooked me up with this guy. Of course, he played the game acting like he was my man until the pimp came out. He said, "Babe, I know a way we can make some money." He couldn't afford motels anymore, so he moved me into this home up on the hill, Kelly Hill. I didn't know he wasn't alone. He had a girlfriend and a son living with a lady that smoked dope. I guess that is how he paid his rent, supply and demand.

Pimpy sold me a dream. He said, "Baby, we can do this." Pimpy went to buy me clothes, giving me a new look saying, this is fifty-fifty. I get half, and he gets the other half for him being my "protector." I don't know what I was thinking. I had nothing to lose. I couldn't get in contact with Mother again. She left the states. So, I went with the plan Pimpy had.

Pimpy and his cousin were pimping a white girl too, so he took us out to San Francisco, the Bay Area, on the strip. I thought, "Wow! I'm really doing this. What the fuck am I doing?" I remember walking up and down the block. My pimp telling me when another pimp looks at me to put my face down, don't say a word. Because if I do, I'm choosing. Plus, he was trying to keep a count on how much money I was making. A lot of times, I would hide in the coffee shop because I didn't want to sell my body. Other times, when I did catch a trick, I would keep some money, but we all know that didn't last long.

One day San Francisco Police Department did a sweep. The paddy wagon came through, and I was one hoe they caught. Being arrested was the scariest feeling I had ever felt. They let me go with a warning, and when I returned home, Pimpy didn't believe me. He thought I was with another pimp or hiding money, so guess what comes next...slap. He hit me! Of course, Pimpy apologized, and I fell for it. Ass whooping after ass whooping with wire clothes hangers until I swore that was the last time. I finally woke up. It was the final beating that changed my life.

Pimpy set me up and put a hoodwrink covering over my head and threw me in the car one night. I was so scared. I remembered when the car stopped, Pimpy and his crew began to beat me until I couldn't move. Then Pimpy took the hoodwink off, saying, "He had to put fear in me." That was it for me. I acted like Pimpy taught me a lesson. He took me to The Track. The reason why this particular area was called "The Track" was that it was known for pimps named "Tennis Shoe Pimps." They would chase hoes up and down the strip. This was a perfect time for me to act like I had chosen and then get the hell on.

Well, I was back to being homeless. I found a homeless shelter in Oakland, California, and got a job at a local soul food café down the street from the shelter. I remember feeling good being able to have a little money in my pocket. I was working as a waitress, nine to five were my hours, but one evening I got off of work and I was really tired walking across the street, and an SUV pulled up. I froze. My OG from around the way, my attacker, my rapist, jumped out and chased me, saying he was going to kill me for telling he raped me. I was screaming, so he left me alone because of the attention I was drawing. Still shook up, I walked to the shelter. My heart was racing as I began to have flashbacks. The abandoned building, the striping of my clothes being torn off, the act. Him telling me if I run, he would kill me and burn the house down with me in it. My heart sunk.

Some weeks went passed, and I met a man from Georgia. Real quiet, a resident at the shelter who was also down on his luck. The shelter was a type of place that helped you get back on your feet. He and I started talking. We became close, eventually moving out of the shelter into a studio apartment in downtown Oakland. That's when things changed. He wasn't my knight in shining armor but my worst nightmare.

SHADOWS FROM BEHIND

Chapter 5
My Worst Nightmare

Things were going good—me and Shorty against the world. I had a little gig, and Shorty had one too, but I started noticing some changes in his attitude, a possessive, jealous spirit. I remember we were at the DFACS office getting our benefits, some food stamps, and I ran into an old friend from the Chabot Junior College, where I attended briefly. His name was Jack, a white guy we had a math class together. Anyway, he spoke to me and I to him. After we spoke and had a short conversation, we departed. Shorty went ballistic, asking, "Who was he?" continually asking a thousand and one questions. As I was explaining myself, I began to see this rage in his eyes blocking me out. When we got home, I was walking to the kitchen when Shorty slapped the mess out of me talking about, "I disrespected him." Well, of course, he apologized, but we all know that wouldn't be the last time he would hit me.

Times were getting hard, so Shorty asked me if I wanted to move to Georgia with him, stating he was from Atlanta and he had some people that could help us out. Not knowing where my ex-husband and children were, I agreed to leave California in June of 1994. Shorty and I left the Golden State and caught the Greyhound bus from San Francisco. In three days, we arrived in Atlanta, better known as "Hotlanta."

When we arrived in Atlanta, thinking we would have a place to go turned into walking the streets, staying at shelters and abandoned houses. I remember sleeping at the Salvation Army down on thirteenth street. To top it off, Shorty was not from Atlanta. He was from Augusta, Georgia. A Busta Ass Nigg...WTF!

Eventually, we got on our feet. I was working at Dunkin Donuts in the Midtown area off Spring Street, and Shorty was working at Greyhound. I remember Shorty and I was hanging downtown underground when we met a group of people that stood out because they were wearing blue flags, so they looked at me also. They approached us, asking where we were from in Atlanta. Of course, Shorty was paying them no apparent attention because he was looking at this thick-ass female across the way. Shorty had the nerve to pick a fight with me so he could go talk to her. You know I didn't see him until later that night.

    I hung with my soon-to-be homies, which one of them later became my baby's daddy. Shorty and I saved some money and soon moved into another studio apartment in Midtown with one of his co-workers. I noticed Shorty was supposed to be working double shifts; I wasn't seeing him as often anymore. One evening, Shorty, me, and my friend had some drinks at a local bar. We had good conversation until something set Shorty off. As all three of us were leaving the spot, I remember walking up the stairs when I felt a kick in my back. It was Shorty. He kicked me in my back, saying, "Fuck me and our blue flag." Well, my friend was like, "What the fuck." and began to help me up.

As time went on, Shorty was still hitting on me. The beatings became more severe as time passed. Shorty went from hitting me in private to hitting me in public. He became more distant, so I began to do some snooping, and guess what I found? Some letters from another female, someone he worked with. Shit hit the fan. I told him I wanted to leave him. Shorty attacked me physically and sexually. He put a pillow over my face and a butcher knife at my throat. I called the police and my friend. The attack was more than an attack. Shorty raped me! I remember when Shorty was done, he had a blank look in his eyes.

Atlanta Police Department came and arrested Shorty, later releasing him. What I learned is if you stay with a person/boyfriend, the system doesn't take you seriously. At this time, I had got close with my friend soon-to-be father of my twin girls. Later, I learned of another disappointment. I went from out of the frying pan into the fire.

Chapter 6
Out of the Frying Pan, Into the Fire

The first six months were good. Once again, back homeless, staying in hotels and motels. My friend, Blue, took me in with his Big Mama and family. I was working off and on as well as him. We soon moved out and moved in with some of our homies. We shared the responsibilities with rent and bills, but we were making minimum wage. One of my homegirls, Queenie, was a stripper. Back then, we called dancers "Shake Dancers." Well, Queenie told me I had a pretty face and shape, and I needed to take advantage of what I had. I used to see all the money Queenie was bringing home when I was rooming with her. I was curious, but I didn't think of stripping, but that soon changed. I ran the idea past Blue, and he had no problem with it. Of course, he saw dollar signs.

I remember going to the strip

club, and the manager asked me to take off my clothes. He looked me up and down and said, "Go get your dance permit and come back the next night." At this point, we were six months into our relationship. That's when it was a change. Blue was starting to be a womanizer. The cheating began.

One night we were at the strip club. Yeah, Blue made sure he was there watching me. Here we go again. Blue started hanging around these want-to-be pimps, who were identical twins. All of a sudden, Blue wanted to be a pimp. I was hurt about the thought of this man that I thought we were down like four flat tires had flipped the script. Blue started hanging out, and I didn't see him for days. Blue talking about, "He gotta go handle some business." We all know what kind of business.

One night, I was in the dressing room getting ready. I was the next booty on duty, so I went to the back of the dressing room where the club's house mom, as we call her, had various items that the gals may need. When I approached her, it looked like she had seen a ghost. I was wondering what was wrong. I thought she had smoked a bad crack rock or something. Well, I finished getting ready and went out on the floor to shake what my mamma gave me. Here comes the club manager, Paul, aka Stiff Mouth. His mouth was always twisted because he burnt out his nose snorting cocaine, so he started putting it in his mouth. He asked me for my bar fee, a fee that the dancers had to pay, a house fee before dancing.

So, as I was walking towards Paul, he told me to go to the office. It was funny because it seemed like all eyes were on me for some reason, and why couldn't Paul take the money right there. A co-worker of mine said, "Don't go in the office." So, of course, I opened the door, and what do I see? Blue with his hand around this bitch waist. It looked like they were about to turn up.

The funny part about it was she was a hoe; Stallion was her name. She already had a pimp, and the pimp had a stable that worked at numerous clubs.

When I saw him and her, I snapped. Blue was trying to explain it wasn't what I thought. By that time, I went back to the dressing room, trying to fathom what I just walked into. Picture the dressing room. It was two parts of the dressing room: one part was bitches puffing on hay or weed, and then it was the other part, bitches sniffing, getting high. I was so heated that I asked somebody to give me a bump. Bitches looked at me like, "Did she say that?" I was a square chick in some ways until then. Someone always told me, "Don't let anyone turn me out," and I always said, "If that happened, I would turn myself out." So, here we go.

    I took a line of cocaine. The next thing I knew, I went on the dance floor, the next booty on duty. Blue was watching me, and Stallion was sitting in the DJ booth with this DJ, who she was fucking. I felt numb as fuck. All I remember was I walked up to her and snatched her ass off the DJ booth. The speakers fell, and I began to whoop off on her ass. I remember six men pulling me off her. They broke it up, and Paul called me in the office. She had the nerve to be hiding behind the other part of the office. I still wanted that ass, but Paul suspended me for three days. That was okay. I had some money put to the side, and I brought me some flake, cocaine, and took my behind home. Come to find out, Blue started snorting before I did. That explained a lot. This was the beginning of a long battle with "white girl."

SHADOWS FROM BEHIND

Chapter 7
Mistake After Mistake

Things didn't get any better. Between the nights I worked at the club and the private bachelor parties, all I saw was glam and the mighty dollar. These parties were full of horny ass men, drugs, and extras. That is a nice way of saying tricks. It would be ballers that come into the club and picked girls to leave with them. Pay bar fees and give dancers their money upfront. Anything that you made, like tips or extras, was yours. I'm not going to lie; I loved the glamour and the lifestyle. I felt important, or that's what I thought. Well, things got worst. Blue was basically depending on me. One time, I let him hold my money. I had made a decent amount one night, and it was slow in the club, so when he picked me up, I ask him for my money. We had to pay for the hotel we were living in on the Southside East Point on Washington Road, Mark Inn. Guess what Blue told me? He doesn't have it. I was like,

"Where is the money I gave you?" Blue said he spend it on flake. "I lost it! I was whooping that ass around West End train station. I had plenty of days like that. Blue saw that I was holding out, so he went into pimp mode talking and fucking other girls, etc. but, of course, Blue said, "It's all business."

In between Blue hitting on me and me hitting on him, we got pregnant. I remember when we found out, I came out of the hospital speechless. Blue looked at me, asking, "Are you?" I said, "Yes." It wasn't one baby, but two. We both were looking crazy. All I knew was I had to stop dancing and drugging. We all know the drugging was harder than the dancing. No income coming in, so we eventually moved in with his people. I was there, and Blue wasn't. When that burned out, we went from home to home.

Eventually, we had a place to stay. I felt stable even if it wasn't our own. It was one of our friend's mothers, Mrs. Knight. She was nice, like a mother figure to me. Something I longed for. I had my twin girls. After the birth and healing, I went back to the life. That's when Blue called himself breaking up with me, resulting in my babies and me being homeless, going from shelters to shelters. My stupid self, still meeting up with him. Still sleeping with him, thinking that we could be a family again. That wasn't in God's plan.

Eventually, I moved into a rooming house—my twin girls and I against the world. When Blue heard I was trying to get back on track, of course, he tried to come back into the picture. I was still messing around with him, but at this point, I was doing me. His family helped me with the twins while I went to work back to the club. Blue became less and less important. Someone else caught my eye that would later become my soul mate, my husband.

I became pregnant again. This time I was unsure who baby it was. I really believed it was my baby's daddy, and Blue thought so too. Same routine. Stopped working and staying with his folks. See, the last time I saw Blue was when he went to the Caribbean to smuggle dope back into the US. I begged Blue not to do it, but Blue went anyway, leading to a ten-year sentence—three years in prison and the remaining time on parole. I was on my fifth baby while still staying with his folks.

After I had my new baby girl, I took her to the jailhouse, so Blue could see her for the first time. The visit was awkward. See, I still had feelings for this man even though I knew he wasn't about shit, but this was my baby's daddy. So, I planned to go see him again, but when I arrived at the jail, Blue had another female up there too. *Still the same old Blue,* I said to myself. I had enough. Well, I went back to working.

I remember I was looking fly one day when I got off the bus. It was the summer of 1997. As I approached the door of the club, guess who was standing there looking at me?

Chapter 8
The Turning Point

I couldn't believe who I saw, my old fling around the time I had got pregnant almost a year ago. Darrell was working security standing there looking good. Darrell was staring at me with this look on his face like he was undressing me. As I walked past him, we made eye contact. Darrell said, "How have you been?" I replied, "I'm good, Big Daddy Doughlicious" It was a nickname I called him when we used to get busy. I was looking through the glass mirrors on the wall at him to see if he was still watching me, and guess what, he was.

Walking into the club brought back so many memories, good and bad. I saw old and potential clients. As I walked to the dressing room, men were flagging me down, asking when was I coming on the floor. I smiled and said, "I'll be out in a few." Of course, I had to get divalicious.

I opened the dressing room door saying to myself, "The same game, different bitches," as I laughed to myself. I put my dance bag down, did my usual routine. Outfit, check. Heels, check. Make-up, check. Smell good, check. Everything was looking fabulous, but I was missing something, a fat sack of that white girl. I asked around the club and ran into a bitch I used to get high with, still in the game. She knew who had it. So here we go.

I took a couple of one on ones and ordered a shot of Hennessy, ready to go make some money. Feeling good and looking good, I went to the DJ booth, signed in, and looked who could be the first sucker I could get the cheese from, scoping out the scenery. I did a couple of dances. A new face on the scene, well, that is what they thought by this time. I had worked at least four different clubs. I had to switch it up.

It was still early in the evening, so I sat down, looking around, and saw Darrell watching me. I smiled, trying not to look thirsty since I was also watching him. Darrell had started to play with me, taking my costumes and hanging them up while I was table dancing with my clients. Basically, we were having fun together. Something that I was not used to eventually turned into a friendship.

I remember one night, Darrell asked if I needed a ride home. I told him I did, so he opened the door, a perfect gentleman. The staff was watching as I got in the car, *nosey-ass people.* The ride home was quiet at first, then Darrell asked was I seeing anyone. I told him my situation. We began to get close as the weeks went past.

I was still staying with Blue's people; he was still locked up. I guess he got wind I started talking to someone else. Blue started to call the club looking for me. He called numerous times, calling himself checking up on me and my money. As Darrell and I got closer, he finally asked me about my baby girl. He knew he had sex with me around the time I got pregnant. I insisted the baby girl was Blue's. That is what I believed in my heart, so as time passed and finally being intimate, Darrell told me he was serious about me and was in this for keeps. Darrell's exact words were, "You know you fucked up, right? Once you gave me that ass, it's a wrap. You're mine."

I had no issue with that. I was feeling him too. Darrell was eight years my senior. He was of a different breed, not what I was used to. Darrell began spending time with my girls and me every day. We became a family instantly—my three girls and his four kids, one that he had helped raise from a prior relationship. Darrell encouraged me to go back to school and leave the life. He always used to say I didn't fit in. That life was not for me. I was still staying with Blue's family, which came to an end.

See, they saw me not going to the club as much bettering myself, not putting out money every night buying pizza, etc. One night, I went home, and they informed me I need to get my shit and move out. So, I did just that. Darrell immediately moved me out, and since I had nowhere to go, he moved me in with him. But come to find out, he wasn't staying alone.

Darrell was trying to move out of his mother's house, so we stayed there and then moved out into our first apartment together. We both were out the life. I was working at a hotel, the Hyatt Regency, and Darrell had a legit job too. We were maintaining. I still kept in contact with Blue's people. I would let the girls go over there some weekends.

A year into our relationship, Darrell asked me to marry him, and I accepted. We were madly in love. Darrell and me against the world. That's what we would say. So, in July of 2000, we got married—my prince charming. It wasn't a big wedding, but it didn't matter. We were married! That's when trouble came back.

SHADOWS FROM BEHIND

Chapter 9
Trouble This Way Comes

Soon after we were married, Blue got released from prison, which I already knew because his people told me. I told Darrell. He and I agreed to meet Blue over at his aunt's house since that is where he resided. I remember when I was talking to Blue, he had this look like, *damn this bitch really moved on without me.* Darrell was telling him he was not there to take his place as the girls' father. Blue had to understand I had moved on, let's face it; Blue had always had an eye for the ladies. He had females waiting on him anyway. I worked with Blue taking the girls over to his aunt's house on the weekends to see him, trying to do the right thing. I even tried to work with Blue regarding child support, which he agreed to. Darrell, now my husband, took both of us down to the funeral home which had a notary to get our agreement notarized.

Everything was going well until the beginning of the year 2001. Blue's ankle monitor came off, and he went back to the same old baby daddy. Blue stopped spending time with the girls saying he was busy. The little child support stopped. It wasn't like I was asking for much, fifty dollars every two weeks. Amongst dealing with Blue's stupidity, I found out, Darrell and I, were pregnant with our first baby together. That's what we thought. When I told hubby I was pregnant, he told me that he didn't want the baby. I was devastated. He wanted me to get an abortion. I put my feelings to the side and made the appointment at Grady to abort our baby. The nurse told me I had to wait until I was almost three to four months so the embryo/fetus could be big enough so they could abort all the parts without leaving anything behind.

At the end of the day, I made the final decision to go through with the abortion, hoping Darrell would eventually change his mind, which he didn't. It was a decision that would haunt me for many years to come. Darrell and I wanted to go out that weekend, but something didn't feel right. Instead of going with my first instinct, I called Blue to see if he could get the girls anyway. So, I took the girls over to spend the weekend with Blue. I would call to check up on the girls like usual, but this time Blue never answered the phone, and when I left messages, he never called me back, which was odd. Something he would never do.

Sunday, Blue finally answered the phone. It was time for me to pick the girls up, but Blue told me to call before we came, which again was odd. Well, we went to pick the girls up. When I arrived, I got out of the car, and went to knock on the door, I heard my girls in the house, but no one came to the door. So, I began to bang on the door harder. Blue finally came to the door and said, "I called the police on your husband. He has a warrant out on him for cruelty to children." My heart stopped. I screamed to Darrell that Blue took a warrant out on him. Darrell began to panic. We didn't know what was going on. I thought to myself, "That dirty bastard trying to get me back." Then I began to think, how? Then I remembered, Darrell had chastised one of my daughters one evening. She had some old marks on her, nothing unusual of a child squirming when getting a spanking. Blue saw the marks on her and ran with it. Blue told me, "I told you no other man was going to raise my girls."

The police arrived and put Darrell in the police car. My girls and I were crying as the police drove off. I called Darrell's mother and told her what happened. So, she came to drive us home. At this time, Blue had his ass on his shoulder. He thought he had the world in his hands. Blue thought we would get back together. I thought to myself, "You went after my family, the man who took care of your girls while you weren't around." Blue called himself, getting back at me.

A bond was set, and Darrell was released. As time passed, Darrell and I went back and forth to court, dipping and dogging to see each other. One of the stipulations regarding his bond was

Darrell, my husband, could come around two of the girls but not the one in question. Finally, after going to court, the judge came to a decision. The lawyer convinced him to plead guilty, and since it was his first offense, he would not do any time but would complete time on paper. The First Offender's Act, something that was blown out of proportion, was later expunged off Darrell's record. This started years of animosity and bullshit to come.

At this point, Blue wanted a paternity test for Baby Girl, our last baby, since I put him on child support. We went to court, and they said the results would come in the mail, and the results were...

SHADOWS FROM BEHIND

Chapter 10
Shit Just Got Real

Blue was not the father! My heart sunk, but at the same time, I was relieved because he was a deadbeat anyway. Blue was not in the girls' lives by his own accord, so Baby Girl wasn't missing anything. I remember sitting at the bottom of the bed after opening and reading the paternity results, thinking the only possible person was, OMG, my husband, Darrell.

My mind went back to Darrell and our "escapades," as I called it. He was the only other person I was sleeping with. I thought I should bring this to his attention. It probably won't be a big deal because he always thought in the back of his mind, he was Baby Girl's father because of the timing and Darrell and her bond from the start when she was six weeks old. I brought it to Darrell's attention, and to my surprise, he said, "Good," before I could get it out of my mouth. Darrell said, "Let's get a paternity test." So, we did, and six weeks later, the results came back. Darrell was the father of Baby Girl. God definitely works in mysterious ways.

As years went passed, Blue and I went back and forth to court for child support, or, as I call it, kangaroo court. I had to beg this man to take care of his responsibility. Every time we went to court, his sorry ass stood before the judge. Blue always had an excuse, "I can't find a job." It's a damn shame the court has to get involved to make a man take care of his children.

For several years to come, that was Blue and I's life, trying to make him visit and spend time with his girls. It went from court-ordered visitation, his ideal stating I was keeping the girls from him to I see them when I see them. Blue's women, drugs, and the life, was more important than his children. He had the nerve to open his mouth and say to me, "Your husband is supposed to take care of them. That's his job," because we were married. So, guess what, that's exactly what Darrell did. A year later, Blue was mad because the girls called Darrell daddy.

Besides the baby daddy drama, Darrell, me, and the girls were living the life. Outside of the everyday struggles, good and bad, we were in a good place until I found out I was pregnant again a year later in the same month. I remember I was at the hospital, and they gave me the results, positive. My first thought was of happiness, and then I thought, what about Darrell's reaction. I automatically went back to the first abortion, which was a dark place that was still in me that I didn't deal with. So, I gathered the courage to tell Darrell, and his response was, "Okay, what do you want me to do about it?"

Darrell's voice was so careless this time, I was feeling a sense of emptiness. I decided to abort another baby we had while married, all in the name of pleasing a man and not doing what was right for me. Again, I had to wait until I was about three months pregnant so the doctor could vacuum all of the parts of the baby, leaving nothing behind. I was getting attached to my baby, going through the morning sickness again, I hoped Darrell would change his mind, but he didn't. He still wanted me to get an abortion.

I remember that morning around six a.m. my mother-in-law dropped me and Darrell off at the hospital. We checked in. I was looking at the other women there, also thinking to myself, *these girls, some strippers, that got pregnant by their tricks, or girls that just felt some kind of way—the ghetto life.* Here I am married, and I have a husband that doesn't even want our baby.

The nurse called my name for registration. She asked me was I single or married. When I said, "Married." She looked at me with sadness and said, "You're married, and you're getting an abortion?" I said, "Yes," and signed the papers. I went back into the waiting room as Darrell was sitting there with me. I had a sense of numbness. They called me back to the surgical room. I remember music playing. The nurses gave me Motrin for pain, but nothing could compare to the pain aching in my soul.

As the doctors were performing the procedure, I felt the vacuum suctioning my baby out of my womb. I began to cry. It wasn't because of being uncomfortable but condemning my soul. I remembered the nurse rubbing my head as I was glancing at the tube sucking tissue out of me and something snapped inside of me. The abortion was finished. Darrell was waiting in the waiting room. My husband, who was supposed to protect me, but instead did the biggest harm to my spirit. I began to cry. That was the last abortion for me. It did something to my soul which brought me back to old playgrounds. I started back getting high.

SHADOWS FROM BEHIND

Chapter 11
Oh My God

Darrell being of Christian faith, which is the majority in the South, went to church from time to time. Being raise Methodist, he asked me if I wanted to go to church with him. We got married in the church, but that was as far as it went for me being raised in Islam. The few times I did go, it was just to go through the motions. Darrell's mother's church was the first church I ever went to, honestly. I didn't feel anything like the Holy Spirit or any connection to God. As soon as my Christian journey started, it ended. That too came to pass. I was still curious about Christianity, so Darrell and I, both as a family, started visiting other churches. Some churches I liked, some I laughed at, and others I didn't like. But one day, everything changed.

I was attending a church that sat on a hill. Not a small or large congregation. It was just right. I remembered the choir singing "God's Trying to Tell You Something" off *The*

Color Purple soundtrack. It was a movie I could identify with because of a character named Celie, with which I, too, had similarities. I always felt that song, but it was different this time. Something came over me.

As the choir started to sing, "Speak Lord, speak to me," my flesh began to get goosebumps. I began to feel weak. My throat felt choked up, and I began to cry. For the first time in my life, I began to feel. From that moment on, I started attending the church on the hill on the regular basics. Finally, my family and I joined the church. Things began to change for the better in my life. I went back to school to get my GED. I passed with high scores in science, literature, and arts. I also enrolled in an office technology course, which I became certified in Microsoft Office Software that opened doors in the job market for me.

I landed an office administrative assistant job which I enjoyed. In my spiritual life, I became active in the church. Darrell and I became active in the adult choir, and the girls joined the children's choir. We enjoyed being active in the Lord. I began to feel like a human being, a person that feels and has emotions, but it was just the beginning of my journey of spiritual warfare. Demons I had buried so deep that it would not just take a year, but I would deal with many years to come.

God's mercy blessed me with yet another job opportunity. I landed a job with the county as an administrative assistant. God placed me in the right place around the right people. He was working his grace and mercy because something I thought would never happen to me evolved.

I had a co-worker who I told my story regarding my mother, not knowing where she was. I guess she was touched and began looking for my family. One afternoon, while waiting to get off, she, who I now call my angel in disguise, looked up my great uncle. I didn't know at that time what she had done. I answered my phone at my desk and guess who it was? It was my great uncle, my mother's uncle on her father's side. He was like a father to my mother. He raised my mother and aunt. When I heard his voice, and he told me who he was, I began to cry. I couldn't believe after so many years, from the age of fifteen to thirty, I heard from someone.

    Uncle informed me a young lady from my job called him and told him she knew someone who was looking for her family. My co-worker, my friend, my guardian angel to this day, I will be forever grateful. Friend, if you are reading this book, you know who you are. Thank you! I was so emotionally drained, my supervisor, after me telling her what happened, let me leave early, but before that, my uncle asks me where had I been all these years. He informed me my mother was supposed to call me that evening. My heart stopped.

Chapter 12
Family Reunion

So, I rushed home with so many different feelings going through my mind. I was wondering how my mother's voice would sound, what will she say, etc. When I got home, I told Darrell of the great news. He was very happy for me. I got the girls settled, cooked dinner, and helped them with their homework then the phone rang. I looked at the number it was an 856 area code. My hands were sweating, so I picked up the phone and said, "Hello." It was a voice on the other side that replied, "Asalamalakim Alaykum, nigga! What's up with you?"

I was so surprised to hear my mother's voice I just started to cry. Mother went on to ask where had I been, what has been going on with me, etc., like we were friends and just doing some catching up. I asked where she and the family were, and did she try to find me. Mother replied, "Why didn't I try to find them. If anything, you should have been looking for me." Furthermore, she said, "I must have been living some kind of way—living foul. I knew not to bring that shit around her. I didn't want to be found."

As time went past, I still felt like that little girl. All I wanted was for my mother to love me. We talked on the phone again like we were girlfriends catching up, not as a mother with concern, or taking responsibility for the damage she had done to my soul. Continuing with my life and my relationship with my mother, I really didn't talk to my siblings. I kind of got used to this relationship, if that is what you would call it. I was just happy I had my family back in my life.

I received a phone call one evening. I remember just like it was yesterday. When I answered the phone, it was a voice I wasn't familiar with, but this person called me Muff Muff. It was my favorite auntie, my daddy's sister, who helped raised me when I was little, living with my grandparents. OMG! I couldn't believe it. I answered, "Yes!"

and began to cry and my auntie too. Auntie began to ask me multiple questions, "How are you. Where have you been?"

She began to explain what went down back in the day. Auntie and I talked for hours. It felt so good to have someone give me an explanation and fill me in on my family. I began to tell her what had been going on with me, telling her what happened from past to present. Auntie told me about my grandparents, Big Mama. Bad news. She died two years ago, which was sad. I remember sitting on Big Mama's lap and drinking chocolate milk. Remembering her big hugs, warm smile, and her wigs. Oh, how I missed her.

The last memory I had of my Big Mama was when my mother came and got me from my grandparents' home when I ran away when I was little. She was begging Mother to let me stay. We also reminisced about Auntie and I's relationship. I remember a green and white sundress, to be exact, with jellybean shoes, thick hair, and Auntie combing it ...Ouch. I began to tell her I was going to church and was active in the choir, telling her that I was happy in my life. Auntie was happy for me, and then she began talking about my mother, which was a short topic. Then Auntie began to talk about my daddy, explaining how distraught he was and how his life was without me.

    I've always longed for my father, *my daddy*. Even though my stepfather treated me like his own, it was that little girl in me. It was that little girl in me that missed him so much. In my eyes, I didn't care what my parents did, I just wanted to be loved, and I love them. Auntie told me my dad would be calling me soon, so be expecting his call. The next night, I got that phone call.

Chapter 13
The Truth Comes Out

I was hurt regarding the harsh words coming out of Mother's mouth. I told Mother because of her marrying me off at the age of thirteen, I hated Islam, which later on in my journey, I revisited Islam and learned to love it and understand it for myself. Furthermore, Mother stated, "She didn't owe me shit! She did what Allah and the prophet, may peace and blessings be upon him, said to do."

I told Mother of my hurt and journey thus far that I've been through, and again, Mother said, "So what. I've been through it too."

Basically, Mother did not take any responsibility for the things she caused or put in motion. But now, the place in my life presently is at peace because my trials and tribulations made me who I am now. Mother and I still talked, basically, our conversations were about her issues. I didn't mind, again that is my mother. I know now you can't be mad at a person that doesn't know how to be a mother or affectionate because she herself didn't experience it. You can't show what you don't know.

One conversation, Mother was scared I was bad-mouthing her to my father. I guess it was her conscience because of all she had done or haven't done. Mother went as far as calling Darrell trying to talk about me to him, saying I was a bad child. The funny part about that was how bad was a child at the age of thirteen? Really. At the age of thirteen and I raised myself. Darrell let me know my mother was on the phone, so I picked up the other phone in the house and listened to the conversation. When I had enough, I asked her, "How can you talk about your own child to her husband and, furthermore, someone you don't even like?" Mother tried to explain, but I hung up the phone.

We had planned to go to New Jersey to meet my family and reunite with Mother. Regardless of our falling out, I still wanted to see her and my siblings until Mother said, "You and my grandchildren are welcomed, but that nigga..." referring to my husband, "...is not!"

I was appalled at the statement Mother said. I told my husband about the conversation, and Darrell's feelings were hurt. I called Daddy, telling him about the conversation Mother and I had, shaking my head. I could remember thinking, "What does it matter if Darrell, my husband, comes in the house." Mother stated he is not Muslim, so he couldn't come in. I was like, "It is not about my husband. It's about repairing the family." Daddy said, "Well, Muff, you can still come up here to see me and your other side of the family."

So, it was done. Daddy helped pay for the trip back home to New Jersey. I had so many different emotions going through my head. Disappointed about the choice my mother put me in. I had to choose between them both, my husband or my mother, and father I have not seen since I was small, and then when I was fifteen years old briefly.

I was happy and nervous at the same time.

The family packed up headed to New Jersey. Driving to New Jersey wasn't a drive around the corner. Darrell drove sixteen hours. I love him so much. He knew how much the reunion meant to me, a beginning of healing and closure. As we approached the New Jersey Turnpike, reality hit me. *Wow, we are getting close*, I remember saying to myself. I wished I could see Mother. Why did she have to be so cold? At the same time, I was so excited to meet my father, something I had waited a very long time for.

We arrived in Camden, my city, around eight p.m. Father was blowing my phone up, asking had we made it yet. I told Daddy we were in the city, and he told us where to meet him. *Omg, finally, the time had come to meet my father.* My heart was pounding. I was so nervous trying to remember how he looked. I asked Father what he had on so I could recognize him. As we were approaching, Father replied, "I have on a beige Kango, khaki slacks, and a blue Polo shirt."

Pulling up to the corner store, I saw a tall man, caramel complexion with a smile, looking at me with tears in his eyes. As Daddy began to walk up to the car, my legs froze. I couldn't move. A voice said to me, that is your father, go and be happy.

SHADOWS FROM BEHIND

Chapter 14
Daddy

I ran to my daddy. I remember the feeling I had when I ran into my father's arms. I felt safe, loved, and protected. Like a little girl again. Daddy looked at me and kissed me on my forehead. I said, "I can't believe it's you. I have tried to picture your face trying to remember how you looked." Now we were face to face looking at each other in disbelief. We couldn't do anything but laugh. I began to introduce my family to Daddy, Darrell, my husband, and his granddaughters.

At that time, it was only the twins and Baby Girl. They all were so happy to meet him. Darrell's father-in-law and the girls' grandfather, they automatically took to Daddy. Daddy helped us with our stay. He paid for the hotel room, but first, we went to his home and relaxed a little from the long trip. Daddy was just looking at me and the girls with amazement. He said I had grown up into a strong, beautiful young woman.

Daddy poured himself a glass of Paul Mason brandy and turned on the television, forgetting he had the porn channel on. When he realized what was on, he looked embarrassed and hurried up and turned it off. We talked for half the night. I thought to myself, *I have so much catching up to do*, so I told Daddy we needed to rest. I would catch up in the morning. Daddy had a look of sadness on his face, but he knew we needed to rest, so off to the hotel we went.

In the back of my mind, I couldn't help but think of my mother and family, wishing I could see them but the hurt and my pride stopped me from letting my heart feel. The next morning, I woke up thinking, *am I really back home*. Daddy called me and said he had the whole day planned for us. I was going to meet my uncles, my aunt, and last but not least, my Big Daddy. So, we hurried up and got ready.

We met Daddy at his home and picked him up. So many thoughts were traveling through my mind about time lost. If things were different, how would my life had turned out? Our first stop was to get some breakfast at Golden Coral. I could tell Daddy was a little nervous. He looked as if he didn't know how to strike up a conversation while we all sat down to eat. I was hungry, so I was the first to go to the breakfast bar, and when I came back, Daddy was like, "Muff Muff, is that swine on your plate?" And I replied, "Yes, it is. And it is good too."

Daddy said, "If your mom saw you right now, she would have a fit."

We both laughed hysterically, and everyone else was getting their eat on. After breakfast, it was time to see Big Daddy, my grandfather. Daddy said he sold the house after Big Mama died and moved into a high-rise. As we got close to the high-rise, Daddy asked if I was okay. I was so confused and nervous, don't get me wrong, I was so excited to meet my grandfather again. Everything was so overwhelming, but I was okay. I pulled myself together, got out of the car, and Darrell looked at me and gave a looked like are you going to be okay.

As we walked to the building and knocked at Big Daddy's door, I was wondering what I would say. Darrell and the girls were holding my hand, and the door opened. I saw on the other side of the door an old man with a beautiful smile with glasses that looked back at me. I said, "Big Daddy," and he replied, "Muff Muff." Tears began to run down both of our faces.

We hugged each other so tightly, and I felt so loved which I had forgotten so long ago. I introduced Big Daddy to my family. I remember Big Daddy just smiling at all of us. We walked outside through the garden, where he sat every evening. I enjoyed the Jersey breeze which blew across my face. Daddy was playing with his grandchildren as Big Daddy began to share with me and Darrell stories of his and Big Mama's life together. Tales of times when I was a little girl growing up with my father and grandparents.

Darrell and I listened to Big Daddy intuitively as he gave us encouragement, telling us to hang in there. We were both young, and we had many years to catch up with him and Big Mama. He said, "Back in his day, the man brought the money home and let the women take care of the bills." It seemed simple back in the day. Big Daddy asked what happened to me. The last time he heard about me was when I ran into Daddy many years ago when my first husband sent me back to New Jersey when my first daughter was born.

I began to tell Big Daddy what had happened, bringing him up to date on the events of my life. We laughed, we cried, but we enjoyed each other's company. It's funny how time flies when you're catching up. Well, time was of the essence, so we said our goodbyes until the next day. It was time to go meet my favorite Tee-Tee.

The mood was awkward. I missed my Big Daddy already. I didn't want to leave him, but I still had some unfinished business. Of course, Mother was in the back of my mind.

SHADOWS FROM BEHIND

Chapter 15
A Second Mother

Feeling good with Daddy and family, we jumped into the Tahoe heading to Auntie's house. The girls were talking and playing with Daddy while hubby and I were holding hands, as I felt a sense of wholeness coming over my spirit. As we pulled up at Auntie's house, I felt so excited my heart was racing. As we got out of the Tahoe, the girls said, "Mom, why is the neighborhood so tow up?" I started to laugh and replied, "They don't call it 'Dirty Jersey' for nothing."

Walking up to the door, I smelt weed and the song "Groove Me" by Guy playing loudly. Daddy opened the door, and there was my auntie looking back at me. A slim dark-skinned middle-aged woman with a cigarette between her fingers, with a can of Budweiser next to a cup. Auntie looked up and said, "Muff Muff?" I began to cry tears of joy. So many emotions were going through my spirit. We hugged each other for a minute, looking at each other. Auntie said, "My baby girl is all grown up!"

I introduced my family to Auntie. She was so happy, but at the same time, it was a sense of sadness too. So many years lost. The last time I saw Auntie, I was around eight years old. Wow! So many years lost. But again, all things come to pass.

Auntie had a big dog. I remember the girls playing with him as we sat down and began to catch up. Auntie began to tell me about Big Mama when she died and showed me pictures of me when I was little. I remember looking at my auntie as I was listening to the stories thinking to myself, *she looked very unhappy.*

She threw herself in her work. She was the head nurse at Cooper Hospital and worked there for many years coming straight out of college, but deep inside, I sensed emptiness in her spirit. She had no children of her own. As she continued to tell me about the good ole days, a man came down the stairs. I looked up, and Auntie's whole attitude changed. I asked her who was he? Again, the atmosphere got real tensed, and my aunt replied, "My husband."

He looked at me, and when he opened his mouth, staggering down the last two steps, drunk as hell, he began to introduce himself to my family and said, "I'm the damn man who is in charge, that's who the fuck I am."

Auntie was trying to say what he said was a joke, but we both knew he was dead ass serious. He had the nerve to snatch my auntie's beer out of her hand and told her to go make his plate and to bring him another one. I could see the embarrassment on her face. The humiliation was evident that the first impression I had of her husband was that he was a drunk. Darrell had a look on his face like, I hope I don't have to catch a case up here. Auntie told her husband to get that shit himself and to show some damn respect for her family that are guests in her home. She told me to ignore him. Daddy explained they argued all the time. This was their everyday routine.

At this point, I was feeling some type of way. My Auntie was not the person I remembered her to be. Naïve to the fact I didn't know what she had been through in her life. Auntie offered Darrell and I a beer. Darrell didn't want a beer, but I was more than glad to pop that can wide open and smoke me a cigarette, too, Newport 100's to be exact.

The night was getting late. Daddy said Big Daddy called him. He wanted me and the family to go to church with him, so that was the perfect time to tell my Auntie it was time for me to go. She could tell I felt uneasy about our visit, but I assured her I would see her tomorrow. The family and I got into the Tahoe, and I kissed my daddy and told him I would see him tomorrow. Daddy looked like he was feeling some kind of way, but I was tired, and the girls were tired. I had some plans of my own with my husband if you know what I mean. So, we retired back to the hotel.

Darrell and I put the girls to bed, and we went to the other room. I felt nasty with the smell of cigarettes and alcohol from my auntie's house in my clothes. I told Darrell I needed to take a shower. Taking off my clothes as they dropped to the floor in a trail leading to the shower with the hot steaming water hitting my face and breast, I turned around in the shower. The hot water began to run down my hair to my back, and before I knew it, I felt Darrell's hands gripping my hips, and the rest was history. We made wild passionate love, which we had not been intimate like that for a minute. His manhood was enveloped in my juices, and before we knew it, the time was three in the morning. I wasn't complaining. It was time well spent.

SHADOWS FROM BEHIND

Chapter 16
Regrets

We woke up that Sunday morning getting ready to meet Big Daddy at his home church. I remember feeling anxious, and in the back of my mind, I was thinking about Mother. Deep inside, I just wanted a glimpse of my mother and siblings, but my pride wouldn't let me feel vulnerable. That shit she said had me feeling like it was me against the world. Born alone, die alone. Hell, I made it this far without her, no mother figure in my life. Any attempt I had in the back of my mind to convince myself to go and see her been gone. Back to reality. Staring at that handsome man across the hotel room, I couldn't help it as I was getting ready thinking about me and Darrell's passionate early morning hours watching him as he was shaving in the mirror. The girls were getting ready for our visit to Big Daddy's church.

As we were pulling up to Big Daddy's church, one of the girls asked, "Where was Papa, mamma?" I told them we would see him later that day. We walked into the church, and there was Big Daddy, smiling. He was standing there in a black suit with his Stacy Adams on his feet. Big Daddy was looking sharp! I believe he was a deacon of the church. He said, "There's my Muff Muff and her family."

Big Daddy introduced us to everybody, and I mean *everybody* from deacons, members of the church, to the pastor. I was sitting in the church service when my cell phone kept going off. It was Daddy blowing up my phone. He was texting me asking when church service was over. The first thing that came to my head was, *Damn, let me spend some time with my granddaddy.* I had already felt rushed yesterday when we went to visit. Shortly after the service, Big Daddy asked Darrell and me to stay afterward, plus he wanted me and the family to go out to dinner with him and the pastor. I wanted to, but Daddy showed up at the church. Cock blocking right after service. Big Daddy and Daddy were arguing. He told Big

Daddy we had something already planned, so the decision was down to me, Daddy or Big Daddy.

Darrell was looking at me like spend time with your granddaddy, but I was so confused. Darrell saw the confusion on my face, so he pulled me to the side to talk some sense into me. Darrell said, "Look, babe, you already spent some time with your dad. You should really spend the day with your grandfather."

I told Darrell, "I wanted to, but I had already promised I would spend the afternoon with my father."

In the back of my head, I knew Darrell was right, but I told Big Daddy I promised Daddy I would spend the afternoon with him. But something told me Big Daddy had something special or important in store for me. Big Daddy's response was a saddened, "Okay." I told Big Daddy I would come pass to visit him before I headed back to Georgia.

I gave Big Daddy a kiss on the cheek and told him I would see him tomorrow morning, which would be later on a tragic mistake of mine that I would regret years to come. No time to fret since Daddy got his way. It's time to go. Beeping the horn to get his attention, but something else seemed to have Daddy's attention already.

Daddy was looking like someone on that other end of the phone had made him real mad! He turned around towards me with his left hand waving in the air, telling me to wait a minute, let him finish his call. His body language was telling me he was telling that person where to get off, or he was defending himself. Either way, I knew he was in deep shit. When he hung up the phone, he was trying to straighten up his face like the pimp he was trying to portray himself not to have a care in the world, but I knew otherwise, so I asked him, "Is everything okay?" and Daddy responded, "Yeah, Muff. It's nothing that I can't fix." He tried to assure me not to worry.

Chapter 17
Two-Faced

We were on our way to Daddy's home. He invited Auntie, some uncles, and a couple of girlfriends. See, Daddy told me he always has to have a couple of dames. If one would not do, the other will. Daddy asked if we could make a pit stop before going to the house. Of course, we did that for him. What we didn't know was that it was a drug stop. When Daddy got out of the truck, he tried to be low-key, but game recognizes game. I knew what it was. Hell, when Daddy got back into the truck, I couldn't help but smell that sticky icky bomb bud. I wasn't a big weed smoker, but the way that bud smelled, any weed head would enjoy. The aroma of the Mary J was very strong. We couldn't help but smell it moving all the way through the truck. Hubby was pissed off. He had a look on his face like, "No, this fool didn't."

    We hurried up and took Daddy to the house. When we pulled up, Darrell asked Daddy, "Can I talk to you for a minute?" So, as they talked, the girls and I got out of the truck and went up to the porch. I couldn't help but hear hubby and Daddy's conversation. Darrell told Daddy he didn't appreciate him putting his family at risk with that bullshit. Daddy had a little arrogance in his tone, stating he was sorry that wasn't his intention. Hubby was like he didn't roll like that. I didn't want their conversation to escalate, so I called out to them both, "Let's go. Baby Girl has to pee." So, Darrell and Daddy both shook hands and proceeded to the house. Baby Girl told "Papa," which she called my daddy, she had to use it not knowing if she had to do one or two.

So, I took her to the bathroom and then began to help Daddy with the preparation of the food. Baby Girl was taking a long time in the bathroom, so hubby went to check on her. Guess what? She did number two. How can someone so small have a long turd like that? Lol. Furthermore, she stopped up Daddy's toilet. Thank God he had a plunger. Daddy couldn't help but laugh.

He automatically gave Baby Girl a nickname, Tooty Fruity Stanky Booty.

The mood was calm. The girls were watching cartoons, Darrell was sipping on a Budweiser, and Daddy and I were getting the food ready to be put on the grill. Daddy had some Big Pun playing in the background. I was laughing, saying to myself, *look at Daddy trying to be hip*. Well, Daddy asked me if I would finish with the food while he went to his room for a minute. No problem with me, so I relieved Daddy while he went to handle his business, whatever that was. A few minutes later, Daddy called me to his room. "Muff, yo come here for a sec." I replied, "Here I come, dad."

When I got to the door, Daddy was rolling up the bomb bud in some bible papers, Zig-Zags. Daddy asked me if I wanted to hit it. Well, I'm not going to lie, I wanted to smoke the peace pipe with him, but at the same time, I thought to myself, *how can I get high with my own father?* Daddy saw that I was struggling with smoking with him, so he told me if I felt uncomfortable, go ask hubby if it's okay with him, and like a dummy, I did. My stomach was in knots. I had really fixed my mouth to ask it, so here comes my answer from Darrell, "Who does that? Who gets high with their parent? But if that's what you want to do, don't let me stop you!" I don't know if that was the answer I was looking for, but the hell with it. I went right ahead and blazed it up. Well, back to the cooking.

Company started to arrive. The girls were running around out in the backyard playing, and hubby was standing around scoping out the scene as always. The music was pumping, and Daddy was introducing me to his peeps, my uncles. Two of them arrived, talking about how everyone missed me. As we were all in the backyard chilling, guess who comes through the door? Auntie and her drunk of a husband wilding out. Daddy had to rush to them to break them up once again.

In the meantime, Daddy's phone kept on going off. See, Daddy left his phone on the table. Curiosity killed the cat, so I picked up and said, "Hello," and the voice I heard on the other end said, "Sha Sha?" It was my mother.

SHADOWS FROM BEHIND

Chapter 18
Secrets Come Out

When I realized the voice on the other end of the phone was my mother, I froze and just stood there. Daddy saw me and immediately took the phone out of my hand and said, "Hello," and of course, Daddy started going in on Mother. While all this was going on, it's sad how I felt like a little girl again. It's a sad thing for a person to still have that amount of power over you.

    Daddy hung up the phone and asked me was I okay. The question that was on my mind was, *How long had Mother been calling, and was that the person on the phone with Daddy earlier that Day?* The answers to those questions were all, yes. Daddy told me Mother had been harassing him with phone calls since I arrived in town. He also told me he was trying not to let me know because he didn't want my visit to be ruined. I understood, but in the back of my head, I knew that wasn't the only reason for him not telling me. I felt like he wanted to pay Mother back for all those years she kept me from him.

Darrell came over to see what was going on with Daddy and me. I told him about the mysterious caller on the other end of the phone earlier that day. It was Mother! Well, we went back into the cookout. The atmosphere was jumping, the music was pumping, the spade game was on deck, the weed was in the air, but as I looked around, Daddy and my auntie were nowhere to be found. One of my uncles walked up to me and said, "What's up Muff Muff? What's happening?" I replied, "Nothing much. Just enjoying the trip." But in the back of my mind, I remembered that uncle was the drunk and crack head of the fam. Uncle told me that Daddy was very happy I came to see him, but I wasn't trying to hear that. Where are Daddy and Auntie?

As I approached the back door, here comes the two of them. They looked high, but I thought it was just weed, but when I went to take a puff on the blunt, my auntie snapped. She was about to say something, but my dad stopped her in her tracks. To this day, I wonder what else was in that blunt besides weed.

At that point, I became frustrated because deep inside, number one, I knew I wasn't going to have time to revisit Big Daddy, and number two, regardless of my relationship or lack of relationship with my mother, I knew I should have seen my mother and family. It was getting late in the evening. I knew Darrell was getting tired, we had to pull out in the a.m. to head back to the A, so I told Daddy we were going to head back to the hotel to get some rest.

Daddy was acting like he didn't want me to leave, so he began to get his behind on his shoulder. He told me he wasn't ready for me to leave yet, and when I insisted on leaving anyway, he grabbed my arm. See, Daddy was very drunk, and at that point, I didn't want to be around him, so I snatched my arm back and said to him, "Goodbye!"

The family and I headed back to the hotel. It was a sense of quietness, a sense of stillness in the atmosphere. It was an awakening to me regarding my family. I had a knot in my gut, a sense of nervousness. All kinds of feelings were surfacing. Once we pulled up and entered the hotel room, we started to pack up. As I was getting the girls ready for bed, my phone rang, so I picked up the phone and looked at my caller ID. It was my mother. I wanted to answer, but I didn't. I couldn't bring myself to face her at this point. The damage was already done, so asleep we went.

    The next morning, we woke up, and I had so many different emotions that were all stirred up—some satisfaction, some bitterness. I felt incomplete for some reason, but I pressed forward. I put on my big girl panties and finished packing, making sure we weren't leaving anything behind. As we approached the truck, a piece of paper was on the window. Darrell took the paper off the window and began to read it. It was from my mother.

Chapter 19
Headed Back to the A

Darrell gave the note to me as I read it. Mother wrote, "That was really messed up that you came all the way up here and you couldn't even see your mother and family. Remember, paradise lies beneath the mother's feet always."

After I read the note, I began to think about all the time that was lost. All those lonely motherless years, I had yearned for my mother's presence. My emotions took over me. I couldn't move. I stood there next to the truck with that note still in my hand. Darrell saw the look on my face and asked me was I okay as he was loading the last of the luggage up in the truck. As I tried to open my mouth, my throat had a lump in it. I was so choked up. I couldn't get anything out. The girls hugged me, and Baby Girl said, "Everything is going to be okay." I smiled and told them to get in the truck.

Okay, I said to myself. *Alright, you need to really pull yourself together*. So, I began to dry my face, but before I got into the truck, Darrell put his arms around my waist. At that point, I felt like everything was going to be okay. We got into the truck, ready to pull off but hold up. The million-dollar question was how did Mother know where I was staying and what truck was ours? Darrell and I both ask the question at the same time to each other. Before my mind could wrap around the idea of how she could have known where to find me, my phone rang. It was Daddy.

    I answered, "Hello." In a very dry tone, Daddy said, "Hey Muff, I just wanted to see if you wanted to go to breakfast before you hit the road?" I told Daddy I was already on the road. Of course, I could hear it in his tone he was mad. As I was about to tell Daddy about the note, my other line clicked. It was Mother.

    At that time, I just had to see what she wanted, why she left that note, and in my deepest thoughts, I wanted to connect in some way. I wanted to hear her voice no matter what the outcome would be, and deep inside, I felted a sense of guilt. I told Daddy I would call him back and took a deep breath and clicked over and said, "Hello."

Mother said, "Asalamalakim Alaykum. What's up? That was some foul shit. How in the hell you came all the way up here and didn't even come to see your family and me! I had some gold to give you."

I couldn't believe the one-sided statement. Mother was worried about giving me some gold. My heart went down south. I had so much to say to Mother. The first thing that came out of my mouth was, "Alaykum Asalam. First of all, you told me your grandchildren and I were welcomed, but that nigga was not. You totally disrespected my husband and me. You are stuck on him being Christian and me practicing Christianity that you forget I'm still your daughter. It shouldn't matter what religion I practice!"

Mother replied, "Yo, first off, you need to watch your tone, and yo, second off, I'm your mother, and I'm not going to kiss your ass."

When Mother said that, *click*, I hung up the phone. I had so much rage in me I said out loud, *here we go again. It's all about her.*

Mother called me right back. She blew up my phone, leaving numerous messages until finally, I answered the phone. Of course, Mother was pissed and continued telling me how wrong I was. I had to stop her in her tracks. I asked her why she was calling Daddy blowing up his phone, and then furthermore, "You come to my hotel and put that note on my truck telling me I was wrong for not seeing you, but you were at my hotel and couldn't even knock on my door to see me. Really! But, of course, it's not about me. It's always been about you, Mother."

Mother said, "What note? I didn't write any note. Get the hell out here! Anyway, I don't have to explain myself. When your mind is right, call me," and hung up.

I just sat there hurt but at the

same time, a little relieved because I said what was on my chest. But as I sat there, I thought, *how can a mother reject her own child because of a religious preference or the choice of a husband. How can you not take responsibility for your own actions? How can a mother turn her back on her own? I am her daughter!*

All I wanted was a mother's love. It shouldn't matter what a child's status is in life. You may not agree, but that is still your child, love him or her anyway. Darrell called my name, "Are you still here? Are you okay?" as I was staring out the window, thinking about my own demons that I will soon encounter with my own title as mother with my children.

Well headed back to the A, and the question remained, *who wrote that note!*

SHADOWS FROM BEHIND

Closing Remarks

Life's journeys are valuable lessons. The struggles of my life journey made me who I am today. Character is a part of wisdom. Until we peel away the many layers of ourselves and learn to accept who we are, we will never begin to heal.

The question I always asked myself is, *what is the definition of religion?* What is it really about? My thought on it is I believe in my heart that mankind made a mistake when we began to put a title on how we worship the one true God. God, whatever you may call him, Allah, Jehovah, etc., gave mankind revelation in his holy books through time. I'm not that person who puts other belief systems down. As you have read, I have been on both sides, to each its own.

But what I do have an issue with is when in my story, as in many other stories around the world, when religion becomes a battle. When a family member steps out of the family's belief system and chooses to practice or find one's own way. As a result, the family disowns that family member. Who are we to judge? Who are we to say who is right and who is wrong? I have experienced both Islam and Christianity. My thoughts at first were I didn't really understand Islam for myself because of my experience growing up. I didn't understand the beauty of the religion or way of life as I know now. Probably other members of other faiths feel the same way. As I went through life's lessons, I became more open-minded. It comes down to one's own personal relationship with God.

This book was written to reach someone's mother, niece, daughter, wife, sister, lost souls that have been used, abused, neglected, and looking for love and acceptance in all the wrong places. If I can get through my struggles and am still learning and growing, you can also. I've learned not to ever say never what you wouldn't do, never judge a book by its cover, and always stay humble. I am spiritually awakened— shadows from behind. -Imani Aester

www.ingramcontent.com/pod-product-compliance
Lightning Source LLC
Chambersburg PA
CBHW022156080426
42734CB00006B/455